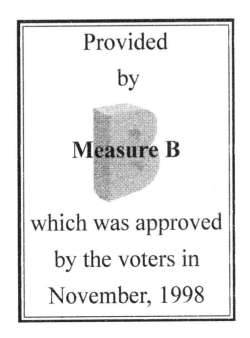

Provided

by

Measure B

which was approved

by the voters in

November, 1998

Learning Is Fun with Mrs. Perez

written by
ALICE K. FLANAGAN

photographs by
ROMIE FLANAGAN

Reading Consultant
LINDA CORNWELL
Learning Resource Consultant
Indiana Department of Education

CHILDREN'S PRESS®   *A Division of Grolier Publishing*
New York • London • Hong Kong • Sydney • Danbury, Connecticut

Special thanks to Alina Perez for allowing us to tell her story.

Also thanks to Dr. Espinoza, principal of Pilsen Academy, for letting us visit, and to the wonderful children in Mrs. Perez's classroom.
  In addition, Mrs. Perez would like to thank all those who have helped her get to where she is today.

Library of Congress Cataloging-in-Publication Data
Flanagan, Alice.
    Learning is fun with Mrs. Perez / written by Alice K. Flanagan ; photographs by Romie Flanagan ; reading consultant, Linda Cornwell.
        p.   cm. — (Our neighborhood)
    Summary: Text and photographs follow a Cuban American kindergarten teacher through her activities as she helps the children in her class learn.
    ISBN 0-516-20774-1 (lib. bdg.)   0-516-26295-5 (pbk.)
    1. Education, Bilingual—United States—Juvenile literature. 2. English language—Study and teaching—United States—Juvenile literature. 3. Spanish language—Study and teaching—United States—Juvenile literature. 4. Kindergarten teachers—United States—Juvenile literature. [1. Teachers. 2. Kindergarten. 3. Occupations.] I. Flanagan, Romie, ill. II. Cornwell, Linda. III. Title. IV. Series: Our neighborhood (New York, N.Y.)
    LC3731.F53   1998
    370.117'5—dc21

                                                                97-14089
                                                                    CIP
                                                                    AC

Photographs ©: Romie Flanagan

Two, Four, Six, Eight
Red, Yellow, Green, Blue

Learning numbers, colors, letters, and shapes is fun in Mrs. Perez's kindergarten room.

Ever since Mrs. Perez can remember, she has loved working with children.

Mrs. Perez was born in Cuba. She came to the United States with her family when she was twelve years old.

Then she met and married her husband Nelson. They had two children.

After the children were grown, Mrs. Perez went to school to become a teacher.

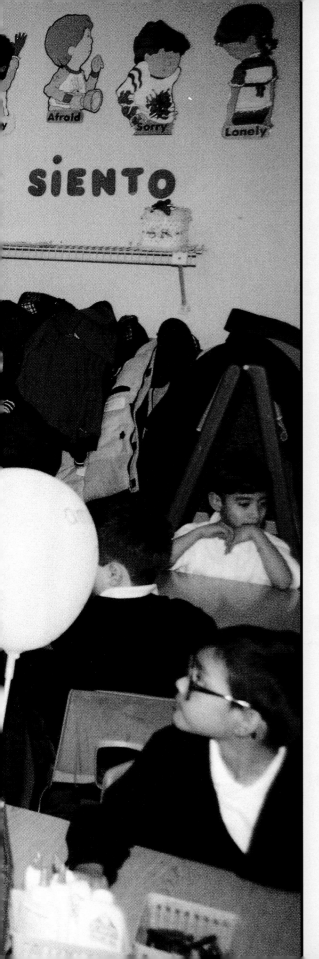

Now Mrs. Perez teaches children. She makes learning fun for her students. She teaches them in English and Spanish, because Spanish is the language they speak at home.

Each morning, Mrs. Perez and
her students talk about the day of
the week . . .

. . . and the weather outside.

Every week, her students learn a
new number

and talk about a letter of the alphabet.

Just before lunch, the students get quiet. Mrs. Perez reads a story or a poem to them.

After lunch, Mrs. Perez lets
everyone play.

Some children work puzzles,

some play house,

and some build things
with blocks.

Then it's time to get into groups to
learn new things. Some students
match letters with their sounds.

Others write numbers that they've learned.

Some listen to stories and try
reading them out loud.

Others count things that are alike
and sort them by color and kind.

Mrs. Perez loves children. In the classroom, she gives them all of her attention. She knows that each one is special and learns in his or her own way.

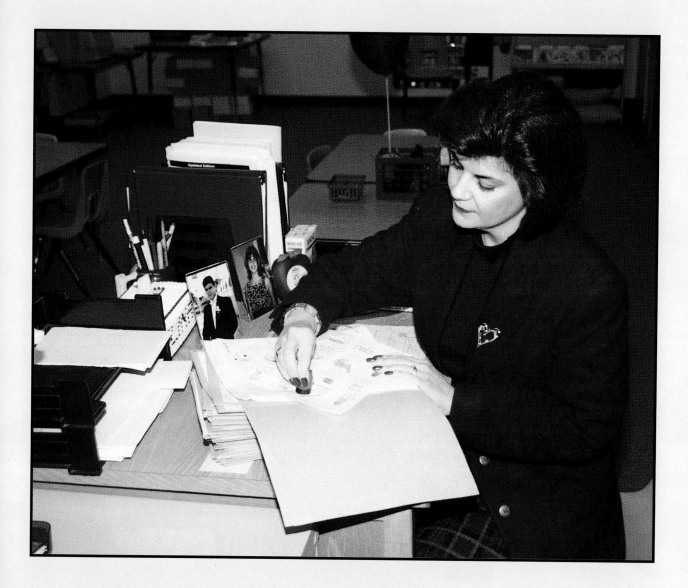

Even when she's not teaching her students, Mrs. Perez is still working.

At home, she plans what she will teach each day and how to make it fun.

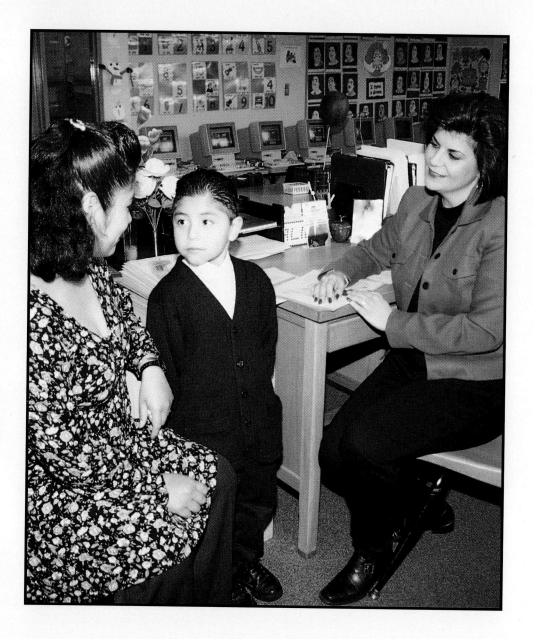

After school, she talks to parents about how they can help their children.

She decorates the classroom and makes it colorful.

At the end of each school day,
Mrs. Perez is tired.

But she is happy, because she loves
helping children learn.

Her students are happy, because they are learning to count and read.

At the end of the year, they will be ready for first grade.

Mrs. Perez is always there for her students when they need her . . .

. . . as a teacher

. . . and as a friend.

Meet the Author
and the Photographer

Alice and Romie Flanagan live in Chicago, Illinois, and have been involved in publishing for many years. Alice is a writer, and Romie is a photographer. As husband and wife, they enjoy working together closely. They hope their books help children learn about the people in their community and how their jobs affect the neighborhood.